The Big Book Of Riddles

300+ Difficult Riddles And Brain Teasers

for Kids And The Whole Family

Dave P. Williams

Table of Contents

Introduction

The oldest known riddle of all time was written more than 4000 years ago and reads: 'There is a house. One enters it blind and comes out seeing. What is it?'. Since man found the evidence of this preserved riddle, they have become some of the most popular educational puzzles amongst both adults and children.

Many children nowadays have video games, cell phones, and television available to keep their minds occupied. However, there are plenty of disadvantages to using these devices at such a young age. For example, it is very easy to become addicted to them, they promote a lack of communication, and they can result in long-term physical damage to the eyes and mind.

For this reason, it is imperative that children find ways to use their brains differently and more productively. One good way in which they can do this is by completing riddles and puzzles that aren't so easy to solve - this will not only improve their problem-solving skills, but it will also lead to a wide range of benefits. For example, riddles improve a person's ability to interpret comprehension, and they can work wonders for increasing a young child's vocabulary.

Experts recommend that children complete riddles in order to expand their minds and improve their creativity levels. However, on top of that, these puzzles can be extremely fun while providing kids with a great learning opportunity.

Riddles are the perfect combination of fun and difficulty. They can leave you feeling frustrated at first, but once you solve them, you will be left with an incredible feeling of accomplishment. More so, riddles are great for creating bonds between you, your friends, and your family - for this reason, you should never be shy when it comes to asking for help from those around you.

In this book, you will encounter long riddles that require plenty of brain-power and problem-solving skills. Don't be scared off by the length, though, as the feeling of accomplishment will be much more significant once you figure them out. We also have plenty of shorter riddles - don't be fooled, though, as these are not as easy as they may sound.

So, if you are a child who is looking to test your knowledge or problem-solving skills, you have come to the right place. We have puzzles of all lengths and difficulties to offer you, meaning that even the smartest of children will be sure to find a riddle that will leave them stumped.

Long Riddles

1. A Japanese ship was moving in the middle of the Pacific Ocean. The captain put his diamond chain and expensive watch on a table, went to take a shower, and continued work ten minutes later. When he returned, both the chain and the watch were gone. The captain quickly gathered his four-man crew.

    The captain asked the British cook about his whereabouts while he was in the shower - the cook answered, "I was in the storage room, selecting meat for lunch".

The captain asked the Sri Lankan housekeeper about his whereabouts while he was in the shower - the housekeeper answered, "I was fixing the ship's Japanese flag as it was upside down.'

The captain asked the Indian engineer about his whereabouts while he was in the shower - the engineer answered, "I was checking to see whether the generator was working correctly.'

The captain asked the French man who also worked on the housekeeping crew about his whereabouts while he was in the shower - the housekeeper answered, "I was sleeping after my night shift.'

After just ten seconds, the captain knew who had stolen his watch and chain. Who was the thief in the end, and how did the captain come to this conclusion?

2. Four men enter a desert. After a while, all of them are knocked out at the exact same time. When they wake up, they find themselves buried to their heads in the sand and unable to look anywhere but dead ahead. They are also positioned in a line, meaning that each man could see the back of the head of another man in front of him.

There is a wall in between the first and second man - this means that the first man can only see the desert and that the second man can only see a wall. The man positioned third from the front can see both the back of the second man's head and the wall. The man positioned right at the back of the group can see two heads and the wall.

Each man wears a hat on their head. The bottom of each of these hats is black, while the top is either white or blue.

Before any of the men can say a word, they are told that if they speak, they will die. However, the first man to guess the color of the top of their hat will be set free. They are also told that two hats are blue and two hats are white.

We know that the order of the hats is as follows: blue, white, blue, white. Which of the four men will be able to know the color of his hat from his position in the sand? More so, why will he be able to know the color of his hat?

3. Sarah was sitting at her study table on a dark night. As her grandfather had just passed away, her parents had flown overseas that morning, meaning that she was completely alone. Even though she was very sad, Sarah had a big exam the next day to study for.

While studying, Sarah heard a loud noise and left her room to see where it had come from. However, as she was looking around, someone suddenly grabbed her.

She tried desperately to break free, but it was no use. The man yelled at her to give him all of her money. However, Sarah cried out, "Leave me. There is nobody at home!"

All of a sudden, the phone began to ring. Sarah asked the man if she could answer the phone, claiming that it was probably her parents and that they would get worried if she did not pick up. The man allowed her to do so but told her not to try anything clever.

Sarah walked towards the phone and picked it up. "Hey Sarah, how is the studying going?" the caller asked. "Hey Lucy, thanks for the call. Do you remember those study notes that I lent you a few weeks ago? I could really use them right now. If possible, would you mind getting them back to me as soon as possible? It is an emergency. I better get back to studying, bye." Sarah then put the phone back down.

"You were very wise not to say anything," said the intruder. He then continued urging Sarah to give him her money. After a few minutes, police sirens could be heard coming up the street, confusing the thief. He let go of Sarah and tried to make a run for it, but he was too late.

How did the police know what was going on in Sarah's house?

4. A father visited his three sons to tell them that he would soon pass away. Since he would no longer be around, he needed to leave his property to one of his children.

For this reason, he decided to put his three sons to the test. He said, "Go to the market and purchase an item that has the potential to fill my entire room, but small enough to fit in a pocket. I will decide who the most worthy is based on the objects that you bring me."

So, all three children went to the market and purchased an item that they believed could fill their father's bedroom and fit in their pockets. Each child returned with a unique object. The father instructed that each son enter his room one at a time to display their gifts and see whether or not it would fill the room.

The first son entered and placed a few pieces of cloth on the floor, hoping that it would cover the entire room. However, it did not. He was sent away.

The second son entered the room and placed some hay that he had bought on the floor. It did not cover the entire room, and he was also sent away.

Finally, the third son entered the room and showed his father what it was that he had purchased. His item did indeed fill the entire room and fit in his own pocket. The father was very proud and claimed that the third child would receive the property.

What was it that the third child bought?

5. Dr. Paul was visiting his cousin Simon at his cabin on the lake. The entire trip was planned so that they could set up Simon's will. Since Paul was Simon's closest living relative, it was understood that most of his belongings would be left to him.

One day, Simon came up to Paul and looked very worried. "Doctor," he started, "I have discovered that a very dangerous man wants to come and get me. He is apparently on his way right now. What should I do, Paul? I have nowhere to hide? I cannot go further into the woods."

Paul took a second to think and then came to a conclusion. He quickly grabbed a 6' bamboo pole that had a diameter of a quarter. "Simon, you must come out to the lake with me. I know that the water is 5' deep, meaning that you will be able to lie on the floor of the lake and breathe through this 6' pole. The man will never be able to find you. When he is gone, I will swim down and find you."

Simon agreed and swam to the bottom of the lake with the bamboo pole. Just a couple of hours later, a forest ranger walked past Simon's house and was shocked to find his body.

Paul told the police everything that had happened, adding that Simon must have panicked and passed away. However, the police arrested Paul and charged him for the murder of his cousin.

Why? (Note: the pole did not have any cracks or holes in it, and the opening was above the water the entire time.)

6. A field that contained many gold mines belonged to a very powerful witch. Not wanting to do it herself, this witch hires one man at a time to mine the gold and bring it back to her. She promises the miners just 10% of the gold that they collect, meaning that she would keep 90% of it to herself.

It is important to note that this witch is blind - because of this, she cast a spell on the three bags given to the miners. The bags have the ability to report how much gold they carried, meaning that the miners could not lie to the witch and take more gold for themselves.

Each man swears to the witch that they will be honest, stating that she can turn them to stone if they are caught cheating. Unfortunately, many men did not know the cunning of this witch - there were many statues scattered around her gold field.

One day, a very honest man named John visited the witch. He quickly accepts her job offer. However, the witch did not trust him. "If I wrongly accuse you of lying to me, then I shall be the one who turns to stone."

On the first night, having honestly done his job, John overheard the magic bags talking to the witch. He decided that he would come up with a plan to deceive her.

The following day, John handed the three bags of gold over to the witch, keeping 1.6 pounds for himself. The witch then discussed matters with her magic bags: the first bag held 16 pounds, the second bag held 5 pounds, and the third bag held 2 pounds.

Angry, the witch accused John of lying and threatened to turn him to stone. However, a few moments later, she was the one who had become a statue.

How did John fool the clever witch?

7. Guslav, The Viking, stayed in a faraway land that contained dragons and sea monsters. However, the dragon population was rapidly growing, posing a threat to the kingdom's safety.

The King of the land was married to Guslav, The Viking's sister, making her his Queen. The royal couple announced that there would be a contest taking place at the end of the week to see who could kill the most dragons from the moment the sun rose to the moment that it set. The winner would marry the King's only daughter, Pavar.

The night before the contest, Gringo, The Gorgeous (the King's firstborn and heir to the throne) went to bed early, planning to save as much energy as possible for the big day. He slept with his sharpened ax next to his bed.

Victor, The Viking, who had nearly forgotten his ax and shield, hiked into the forbidden forest, as he had planned to spend the night there to get a headstart.

Abner, The Able, stayed at home, preparing himself for the long day ahead. He had sharpened his spatha and polished his bronze shield. More so, he had his servant prepare his horse for the competition.

Brav, The Bold, slept in on the morning of the contest and had to rush to catch up with the other contenders.

Igor, The Terrible, was the only contender who used two weapons. He was able to slay 4 dragons with his ax and 5 dragons with his spear by the time the sun had set.

The winner was honored by the King at the celebration dinner that evening. His two parents and his horse were also celebrated because of their valiant son's efforts. This winner had killed more than half a dozen dragons with his ax. The horse of the warrior was also celebrated. More so, his bronze shield was given a spot in the King's hall.

Who was the winner of the contest?

8. Emperor Akbar was the ruler of India for some time. He was very wise and knowledgeable. In his court, Emperor Akbar had the Nine Gems and nine advisors, who were each famous for their special individual skill.

One of the Nine Gems, named Birbal, was known for his wit and wisdom. Birbal was once invited to Persia by the King himself, where he was honored with gifts and celebrations. However, after a few days, he got ready to leave for home.

The night before he left, a nobleman asked Birbal how he would compare the King of Persia and the King of India. He replied, "Your King reminds me of a full moon, while mine reminds me of a quarter moon."

The Persians were satisfied with this answer, and Birbal left for India. When he arrived back home, he was met with a very angry King - It was evident that Birbal's words had made it back to Emperor Akbar.

"How could you say such horrible things about your own King?" he asked angrily. Birbal quickly objected and claimed that he had actually complimented his own King while offending the Persian King. How was this possible?

9. There were once two men, Matthew and Mike, who worked on a construction site. Both men were up for a challenge and formulated an idea.

At lunch, they visited the scrapyard and discussed their plan with the men who had gathered to watch. Mike, who was evidently much stronger than Matthew, started, "We will be having a contest to see who can roll their wheelbarrow the furthest in just one minute. We both have to fill our wheelbarrows with something found in this scrapyard - it can be anything. The only rule is that we both have to start at the exact same time. The loser will have to pay the winner one hundred dollars."

With the game decided, Mike began walking around the scrapyard in search of a light object. However, Matthew did not move. When Mike returned with a small steel rod and noticed that Matthew had not selected an object, he was very confused. Matthew explained his plan to Mike.

After the game, Mike returned home one hundred dollars poorer. What did Matthew do to win the game?

10. On a specific street in England, there are 5 different houses that are each painted a different color. Each homeowner is from a different country, drinks a specific type of beverage, smokes a particular type of cigar, and has a unique pet. It is important to note that none of the homeowners are from the same country, drink the same beverage, smoke the same cigar brand, or keep the same pet species.

The South African man lives in a home painted red.

The Swedish man has 2 dogs.

The Danish man drinks tea as his favorite beverage.

The green house can be found on the left side of the white house.

The homeowner of the green house drinks coffee as his favorite beverage.

The homeowner who smokes Amazon cigars also keeps birds.

The man who lives in the yellow house also smokes Crisp cigars.

The man who lives in the middle house drinks milk as his favorite beverage.

The Norwegian man lives in the first house of the five.

The man who smokes Swiss cigars lives in the house next to the man who keeps cats as pets.

The man who owns a horse lives in the house next to the man who smokes Crisp cigars.

The homeowner who smokes Sunflower cigars also drinks beer as his favorite beverage.

The German man smokes Tiger cigars.

The Norwegian man lives in the home next to the blue house.

The man who smokes Blue cigars has a neighbor who drinks water as his favorite beverage.

Which homeowner owns a fish?

11. There are five pirates who all live on the same ship. These five men have been searching for treasure over the past couple of years. Finally, after deciding that they have enough gold for each of them to live a happy and comfortable life, the five pirates decide to part ways. However, they must decide how they will split the 100 pieces of gold that they had collected.

The pirates decide that the best way to split the gold would be through democracy. Each pirate, from the oldest to the youngest, would get the opportunity to suggest a plan on how to split to treasure. If 50% or more of the votes agree to the plan, that is how they will split the gold. On the other hand, if less than 50% of the pirates agree to the plan, the pirate who came up with the idea will be thrown overboard, not receiving any treasure.

All of the pirates are greedy and want as many of their comrades thrown overboard as possible. The more pirates that are thrown overboard, the more money the remaining pirates will receive.

What plan can the oldest pirate come up with in order to get as much gold as possible?

12. In a faraway kingdom, a King realizes that since he has no sons, daughters, or wife, he must decide who will rule his land once he passes away. After debating the dilemma with his loyal servants, he comes to a very clever conclusion.

In order to decide who will take the throne, the King passes out a bunch of seeds to all of the children in the land. He claims that whoever is able to grow the biggest and most beautiful plant by the end of the year will take over the land once he passes.

The children all gladly accept the challenge and begin nurturing the seeds. At the end of the year, they all gather in the courtyard to display their beautiful plants to the King and his men. The King slowly walks around, closely observing each of the plants.

Once he is finished, he announces to the crowd that he has made his decision. The next leader of the land will be a little girl who failed to grow her seed. She was the only child who arrived in the courtyard with an empty pot.

Why did the King select this girl over everybody else?

13. A businessman leaves an envelope filled with one hundred thousand dollars on his desk at home before he goes off to work. After a long day at the office, the man returns home, only to find that the envelope is missing.

The man quickly thinks about all of the people who had access to his office when he was at work. He has three suspects: his cook, his maid, and the mailman who delivered the envelope.

He calls the cook into his office to ask him some questions. The cook claims that he entered the office and saw the envelope on the desk. He then hid it under a big book in order to keep it safe. They check under the book, but it is no longer there.

He then calls the maid into his office to ask her some questions. She claims that she moved the book to clean the desk and decided to stick it between the first and second pages for safekeeping. However, after looking in between those pages, they realize that it is no longer there either.

Finally, he calls the mailman into his office to ask him some questions. The mailman claims that he opened the book and found the envelope in-between the first and second pages. He then moved it in-between the second and third pages for safekeeping. After opening the book and finding nothing, the man was left stumped.

However, after a few moments, he quickly realized who the thief was and called the police. Who stole the one hundred thousand dollars, and how did the businessman figure it out?

14. A man and his new wife do not have enough money to buy a new apartment after their wedding. For the time being, they decide to move in with the husband's mother.

Upon their arrival, the wife discovers that her mother-in-law has a jar filled with lima beans. This makes her very happy because lima beans are her favorite food. She decides to take one lima bean from the jar every single day that they spend living in the home.

However, their stay went on for a little longer than they expected. The mother-in-law quickly realizes that her lima bean jar that had once been completely full is now only half-full. Although she does not know for sure, she suspects that the wife is the one who had been stealing her lima beans.

One day, the mother-in-law and wife were cooking together in the kitchen. The wife notices the mother-in-law eyeing the lima bean jar and worries that she has discovered her habit of taking a lima bean every day.

Thinking quickly, the wife takes out one more bean and places it on the counter without the mother knowing. At the right moment, the wife picks up the bean and says three words to the mother that completely ease her suspicions.

What were the three words spoken by the wife?

15. Three friends have taken a trip to Mexico to celebrate one of their birthdays. Once they arrive, they check into a hotel near the airport.

   The clerk at reception tells the three friends that the total cost is thirty dollars. With this in mind, each friend pays a total of ten dollars.

   However, after a couple of hours, the clerk realizes that the total bill for the three friends was only twenty-five dollars. He sends the extra five dollars back to the guests with the bellhop.

   Once the bellhop arrives at their rooms, he realizes that he does not know how to split the five-dollar bill between three people. Instead, he keeps two dollars for himself and gives each guest one dollar back.

   Seeing as though each guest paid ten dollars in the beginning but received one dollar back, they each actually paid nine dollars for their room. This means that their total would come out as twenty-seven dollars. However, since the bellhop kept two dollars for himself, the total would actually be twenty-nine dollars.

   What happened to the extra dollar?

16. Two men walk into a restaurant. The one man is wearing a baseball hat, while his friend wears a cowboy hat. They find a seat in the corner of the restaurant and engage in conversation for a few minutes. The man

wearing a baseball hat is seen pointing at the bartender while still talking to the man in the cowboy hat.

After a while, he leaves his seat and walks up to the bartender, claiming that he has a bet. If he can use a water gun to spray water into a plastic cup on the other side of the room, the bartender must pay him one thousand dollars. However, if he cannot do it and messes water all over the room, he will pay the bartender one thousand dollars.

The bartender agrees, and they set the plastic cup up. The man wearing the baseball cap attempts to fill the cup with water, but he messes it all over the room. Laughing, the bartender demands money from the man. However, he quickly notices that the man wearing the baseball cap is also laughing.

Why was the man wearing the baseball cap laughing after losing the bet? Who was the actual loser in this situation?

17. A swan and a dog both live on a farm with a large, circular lake. The swan cannot run very fast, but she is a very good swimmer. On the other hand, the dog cannot swim at all, but he is exceptionally fast on land.

It is important to note that the swan cannot take flight from the water. In other words, she needs to make it to the land before she can fly away from the farm. However, the dog desperately wants to catch the swan, meaning that if she were to swim to the land, there would be a great risk of her being eaten.

The swan needs to come up with a very smart plan. She is in the center of the circular lake. The dog is much faster than the swan is on land, and he is always positioned at the point on the perimeter of the lake that is closest to the swan.

With this in mind, how can the swan make it to the land without the dog capturing her?

18. The police receive a call from a concerned citizen, claiming that they have found a lost child wandering the streets of the town. After a while, the police show up and collect the little boy, bringing him back to the police station with them.

However, the sheriff quickly discovers that the boy is unable to speak, meaning that he will be no help in finding his parents. For this reason, the police announce the lost child to the public, telling the parents of the boy to collect him from the station.

Three couples show up at the police station, claiming to be the parents of the boy. Confused, the sheriff allows each couple five minutes with the boy in order to determine who the real parents are.

The first couple enters the room and spend the five minutes asking the little boy questions and offering him sweets. Once their time is up, the sheriff asks them to leave.

The second couple enters the room and hugs the little boy, claiming how worried they were. Once their time is up, the sheriff asks them to leave.

The third couple enters the room and gives the little boy plenty of toys. Once their time is up, the sheriff asks them to leave.

Who are the real parents of the lost little boy?

19. A newlywed couple plans a trip to Hawaii for their honeymoon. On the third of March, the couple leaves for the airport and, after a few hours of hanging around, they board their airplane.

However, they quickly become scared when the plane starts moving around in the air. Unfortunately, the plane crashes after just a few hours of flying, and every single person on board either passes away or becomes very severely injured.

The airplane crash makes international news. In fact, the story was told on television, in newspapers, and on the radio.

On the seventh of March, the exact same couple is seen walking around the streets of Hawaii. They did not have any scratches, bruises, or injuries on them (they looked completely unharmed).

How was this possible? (Hint: Look very closely at the wording)

20. Johnny is sent to the post office in order to collect a package for his mother. The package contains three hundred dollars, making it very valuable.

On the way to his destination, Johnny runs into one of his friends from school. The friend, named Adam, asks Johnny where he is going. After

Johnny tells him about how he is going to pick up money for his mother, Adam suddenly becomes very interested.

The friends part ways, and Johnny continues on his mission. However, on his way home, he runs into Adam once again.

"I will make you a deal," Adam starts, "If you roll one dice and get 4 or above, I will give you an extra three hundred dollars. If you roll two dice and get a five or six on one of them, I will give you six hundred and fifty dollars. If you roll three dice and get at least one six, I will give you seven hundred dollars. However, if you do not roll these numbers, you must give me your three hundred dollars".

Johnny thinks very carefully about what his friend is offering. He knows that his mother will be very mad if he does not return home with the money that he was sent to collect. On the other hand, she will be very pleased if he returns home with extra cash.

What option should Johnny take in order to stand the best chance of returning home with the money?

21. Three boys share an apartment and have little competitions every day in order to earn money off of each other. One competition that they always have is a raw egg spinning competition.

However, after competing in the same competition every day for over a week, two of the boys decide to call in a personal detective. They claim that the third roommate is cheating in the game as he always wins and steals their money.

Intrigued, the personal detective asks if she can watch the next time that they play the game. Both of the boys agree.

When they compete again, the personal investigator quickly picks up on something odd. You see after the one boy had finished spinning his egg, the maid handed him a broom to clean it up. More so, the maid seemed accustomed to the mess.

It did not take very long for the personal detective to figure out how the boy was cheating in the egg spinning game. How was this possible?

22. Tommy is walking through a dark cave when he comes to a fork in the road - the one tunnel divides into two. He knows that one of the tunnels leads to the land of rewards and that the other tunnel leads to the land of punishment. However, he does not know which is which.

Both tunnels are monitored by a very large guard. The one guard will always tell the truth when asked a question, and the other guard will always lie when asked a question. Again, Tommy does not know which is which.

In order to help him determine which tunnel leads to the land of rewards, Tommy is able to ask each of the guards one question that can be answered with a yes or a no. It is important to note that both the tunnels and the two guards look exactly the same, meaning that there is no way for Tommy to tell which tunnel is which.

Which two questions can Tommy ask the guards in order to determine which one leads to the land of rewards and which one leads to the land of punishment?

23. Two men are running through the woods in order to avoid a rapidly growing forest fire. The wind is blowing the fire in their direction, meaning that they have to hurry in order to escape the flames.

However, they encounter a huge problem when the path that they were following comes to an end. Instead, they are faced with a very large and steep cliff. After further inspection, both men understand that there is no possible way for them to go around the cliff or climb down it.

With no other options, the one man removes his backpack and empties it in order to see what they could use to help get them out of the situation. The backpack contains a single match, a bottle of water, a flashlight, some food, and a couple of berries.

Both men, having extensive survival skills, immediately breathe a sigh of relief. They understand that the objects in the bag can, in fact, be used to help them survive the forest fire blowing in their direction.

After a day, both men walk out of the forest completely unscathed. How was this possible?

24. Mary and Jack are a newlywed couple who have recently planned a honeymoon trip to Croatia. They use a travel company to book their tickets and plan on spending most days at a national park that is famous for its large cliffs.

Once they arrive, they waste no time in visiting the national park. On their third day in Croatia, Jack reaches out to Mary's friends and family, claiming that there has been a terrible accident.

Sadly, while they were at the national park, Mary had gotten a little too close to the cliff and had fallen over the edge. Jack sounded absolutely distraught as he shared the news with Mary's relatives.

The story did not make the news and was kept very silent. However, when the travel company found out about the horrible accident, they immediately called the police, claiming that Mary had not fallen. Instead, they believed that she was pushed.

A few days later, Jack was arrested for the murder of his new wife. How did the travel company know that Jack was guilty?

25. A father and his three sons lived on a very private farm in the middle of the forest. The father would often use his truck to drive into the nearest village. One day, he was in a horrible accident that left him with life-threatening injuries.

All three sons were very concerned about their father and would do anything to save his life. For this reason, they decided to make a deal with the Grim Reaper.

The first son pleaded with the Grim Reaper, begging him to let the father live a little while longer. Feeling generous, the Reaper granted the first son his wish. However, a few months later, he returned to collect the father.

The second son pleaded with the Grim Reaper, begging him to let the father live just a little bit longer. Again, the Reaper decided to be kind and give the family a few more days together. However, a week later, he returned to collect the father.

The third and youngest son begged the Reaper not to take his father. He pleaded, "Give us a few more moments together. I will light this candle, and once the wick has burned out, you can return to take my father." Again, the Grim Reaper agreed.

However, the Reaper never returned to the farm in the middle of the forest. Why was this?

Shorter Riddles

1. Your friends dare you to enter a haunted house on Halloween. Once inside the house, you realize that there are three separate doors at the end of a dark hallway. You are scared of the dark and try using the switch on the wall to turn the lights on. However, you quickly realize that the power is out. Upon further inspection, you realize that the one door contains a bottomless pit, the second door contains an electric chair, and the third door contains a room full of spiders. Which door should you enter and why?

2. Two spies are on a mission to gain access to an enemy camp. In order to be granted entry, they have to give the correct answer to the guard at the gate of the base when he asks them a question. The two men hide nearby,

waiting to hear the countersign given by the guard. The first man comes, and the guard gives the sign: "6". The man answers "3". The guard grants him access. A second man comes. The guard says "12", and the second man answers "6". The guard grants him access. Satisfied, the one spy goes up to the gate. When the guard says "10", the spy answers "5". He is immediately arrested. The second spy who had still been hiding nearby quickly walks up to the gate. The guard says "8", and after the second spy replies, he is granted access. What was the answer given by this spy, and what is the secret code?

3. In a small town called Dorking, there are 2 barbershops. The barbershop in the good part of Dorking is very clean and smells pleasant. The barber is very kind and is always seen smiling. More so, his hair is perfect. On the other hand, the barbershop in the bad part of Dorking is a mess. The entire shop is covered in dirt, and it doesn't smell too great. The barber constantly has a frown on his face, his skin is oily, and his hair is ragged. A new man visits the town of Dorking and asks about the best barbershops around. After hearing about both, he decides to get his hair cut at the shop in the bad part of Dorking. Why does he do this?

4. Before his passing, a father left his will to two sons. In his will, he discussed a stream that his family had used to make money for a very long time. The will also state that the sons could make a single trip to the stream to search for gold. However, they could stay for as long as they wanted, and whoever carried the gold home could keep it. On their way to the gold stream, the sons brought a mule, some food, and a few panning supplies with them. During their stay near the stream, the two

managed to collect and smelt a gold bar that weighed roughly 50 kilograms. However, when they returned home, they couldn't decide who got to keep the gold bar. They took the matter to court, and, after reading the father's will, the judge had come to a very wise conclusion. Who got to keep the gold bar, according to the judge?

5. A woman visits a bank in Los Angeles and takes out a loan for $1,000, claiming that it will be used for an upcoming trip to Asia. The loan officer states that she will only be able to take out the loan if she has collateral. She tells the man that she will leave her car, which was estimated to be worth around $150 000. The bank accepts the car as collateral, laughing at the woman for leaving such an expensive object. After a month, the woman returns and pays back the loan, including interest. The manager of the bank asks the woman why she left such an expensive item when taking out such a small loan. The woman quickly tells him the reason behind her loan, and the bank manager is left stumped at how clever the woman actually was. Why did she take out the loan?

6. Steven was the strongest man in the world. He can lift an object that weighs 1000kg with complete ease. There was a Strength World Cup that all the strongest men in the world entered. The challenge was that they had to lift and hold up an object that weighed 1005kg for six minutes. The winner would be decided by who didn't drop the object until the end of the six minutes. If all the men were able to do it, the judges would give first prize to the man who could lift the object up easily and stand as still as possible. If Steven was the strongest man, he would've come first. However, he came second. Why?

7. Mr. Smith asks, "If I give you one cat, then two more, how many cats would you have?" Michael answers, "Four." Mr. Smith asks him the question again, "If I give you one cat, then two more, how many would you have?" Again, Michael replies, "Four." Mr. Smith then asks, "If I get one cat, then two more, how many cats would I have?" Michael replies, "Three." "Very good job, Michael! Now, if I give you one cat, then two more, how many cats would you have?" Michael quickly answers, "Four." Mr. Smith does not know why Michael keeps giving this answer. However, he is not wrong. Why is this?

8. There is a deserted island with 12 inhabitants. All of the inhabitants weigh the exact same, except for one man, who weighs more. You must figure out who the person is that has a different weight - however, you may only use it three times. It is important to note that there are no scales or weighing devices on the deserted island.

   Which method can be used to figure out who the person is?

9. A woman is staying in a hotel room. While she is in her room, there is a knock at her front door. When she opens the door, she sees a strange man that she has never met before. The man says, "I'm sorry, I have made a mistake. I thought that this was my room." He then walks away and heads towards the elevator. The woman rushes back into her room and quickly calls security.

   What made the woman call security?

10. A farmer passed away and left his 17 cows to be shared between his three sons. The farmer stated in his will that the oldest son would receive half

of the cows, the middle son would receive ⅓ of the cows, and the last son would receive 1/9 of the cows. However, the sons did not understand how they could receive half cows. They sat for many days, trying to figure out how to divide the cows up according to their father's will.

A couple of days later, the neighbor visited the sons in order to see how they were doing after their father had passed away. The sons told the neighbor about their problem, and, after a while, the man said, "I will be right back." He then left again and, when he returned, the three sons could divide the cows according to their father's will.

What was the neighbors' solution to their problem?

11. The Queen of England stays in a stunning castle with her one son and their sheep-dog, named Alex. The Queen decided that she wanted to see her friends, arranging for them all to meet for some tea. When she leaves, she demands that her trusted servants watch over her eight-year-old son. These servants include Harold, Griffith, Tiffany, Philip, Magdalina, Boris, Geraldo, Bernadette, Sandy, Anastasia, Constantine, Joel, Lucy, Sadie, McKenzie, Lawrence, Dorothy, Devon, and Surlamina.

However, when the Queen arrived back home, she noticed that her only son was missing, assuming that he was kidnapped. She insisted that the kidnapper was one of her eighteen assistants.

She interviewed every single servant in order to discover who the liar was. Harold claimed that he was at the gym, Griffith was planting roses, Tiffany was marking homework, Philip was taking photographs of the garden, Magdalina was arranging the bedding, Boris was cleaning,

Geraldo was watching over Griffith as he planted the roses, Bernadette was trimming Alex's fur, Sandy was sweeping the corners of the castle, Anastasia was dealing with royal matters, Constantine was constructing a birdhouse, Joel was writing a few jokes, Lucy was folding the washing, Sadie was making a new dress, McKenzie was playing music, Lawrence was on the phone with the bank, Dorothy was preparing the extract for the Queen's sore tooth, Devon was looking at an X-ray of the Queen's arm, and Surlamina was completing her Secretary of State duties.

Who is the kidnapper?

12. A philosopher forgets to wind up the one clock that can be found in his home. This man had no other devices, such as a television, phone, or radio, that could be used to tell the time.

The man decided to walk down the road to his friend's house. The path to the house was straight and resembled a desert road. He stayed with his neighbor for the night and returned the following morning. When he returned home, he was able to correctly set the time on the clock.

Assuming that he always moves at the exact same pace, how was it possible for the man to know the time when he returned home?

Note: he did not take anything with him to his friend's house, and he did not bring anything home with him.

13. I display a name, but it is not my own. I am used for my longevity. Even though I do not age, I still wither. I always mean the same thing, but I do

not speak. I am planted, but I do not grow. I am not wanted, but I am frequently bought and used. People look at me and see their future.

What am I?

14.   A rich family lived in a round house on the top of a green hill. The mother, father, and two children lived with their maid, butler, driver, and gardener.

One night, the parents were headed into town for a party. They kissed their children goodbye and tucked them into bed. However, upon their return, they noticed that both children were missing.

Suspicious of the maid, butler, driver, and gardener, the parents pulled them each aside to be interrogated.

First, they spoke to the maid. The parents asked what she had been doing while they were out at their party. "I was cleaning the corners of the house," was her reply. Second, they spoke to the butler. "I was putting the leftovers from dinner away," was his answer. Third, they asked the gardener. "I was taking a shower," was his answer. Lastly, they asked the driver. "I was in my bed, watching television," was his answer.

Immediately, the parents knew who was lying. Who was the guilty person, and how did the parents figure it out?

15.   A man owns a fox, a rabbit, and some lettuce. He is sitting on the edge of a river with a small raft, trying to find a solution to his dilemma.

The man needs to get to the other side of the river as quickly as possible. However, the raft is only capable of carrying him and one other object. Without him being there, the fox would eat the rabbit, and the rabbit would eat the lettuce.

How could the man transport himself and all three objects to the other side of the river?

16. Adam is going away for a couple of weeks on a work trip. He lives in an extremely remote area - in fact, the closest neighbor is more than a mile away. However, Adam faces a problem: his area experiences frequent power outages and, if the power goes out too often, the meat in his freezer would go bad.

Adam owns a digital clock and a VCR that flashes 12:00 whenever the power goes out. However, the clock and VCR would flash even if the power only goes out for a couple of seconds.

Adam must find a way to determine whether or not the power went out for long enough to thaw his food while he was away. He cannot ask the neighbor because she lives more than a mile away, meaning that his house could experience a power outage when hers does not. More so, he does not have anyone to house sit for him.

How can Adam solve this problem?

17. There was a girl who always bragged about how brave and fearless she was. In fact, she bragged so much that her friends and classmates often grew annoyed with her. Because of this, they decided that it would be a

good idea to dare her into doing something scary - this would, she could prove her bravery.

The classmates said, "If you want to prove your bravery to us, go to the cemetery tonight. You must be alone, and you cannot take any torches or flashlights with you. When you get there, stand in front of Mr. Gregory's tombstone. Rumor has it that if you stand there for five minutes, a hand will reach out from underground and pull you under with it. To prove to us that you were actually there, take a big rock and place it over the grave. That way, when we walk past the cemetery tomorrow, we will see the rock and believe your story."

The girl agreed and set off for the cemetery at midnight. The air was cold and blew her long dress around, causing her to shiver. Once she arrived, she picked up a very large rock and placed it by her feet. After a few minutes, she began to get scared and decided to leave. However, something was stopping her from moving.

The following day, her classmates passed the cemetery and noticed that there was indeed a large rock at the foot of the grave. However, the girl's body lay next to it.

How did the girl pass away, and what stopped her from running away?

Quick Riddles

1. What 4-letter word can be written backward, forwards, or upside down and still be read from left to right?

2. What kind of goose will pick a fight with a snake?

3. I become more wet when I am drying. What am I?

4. If there are 6 sheep, 3 dogs, and one herds-men on a farm, how many feet are there in total?

5. You answer me when I haven't asked you a question. What am I?

6. What is one word that is always pronounced wrong?

7.   Which 3 letters can scare a thief?

8.   If fish were able to live on land, where would they stay?

9.   What goes up when the rain comes down?

10.   Where is the only place that yesterday comes after today?

11.   What has holes but can retain water?

12.   What do you dig up when dead and bury when alive?

13.   What can be seen in the middle of March and April, but never in any other month?

14.   I am a word with three letters. If you add two more, there will be less. Which word am I?

15.   What can't be kept until it is given?

16.   Which planet was first discovered by man?

17.   What can go up and down a flight of stairs without moving?

18.   What has one head, four legs, and a foot?

19.   What has the ability to grow up while growing down?

20.   What can be filled with empty hands?

21.   I can go through glass without breaking it. What am I?

22.   I lose my head in the morning but get it back at night. What am I?

23. What clothing does a house wear?

24. People sleep the least during this month.

25. What can run around the garden without moving?

26. My head turns from red to black when you scratch it. What am I?

27. What will die if put in water, even though it is made of water?

28. Who has married various women but never gotten married?

29. What object is white when dirty and black when clean?

30. Bring me up, and we can go. Put me down, and we will stay. What am I?

31. What has hands but is not living?

32. The more of me there is, the less of me you see? What am I?

33. You hear me once or twice, and then I die until called again. What am I?

34. If I am as hard as a rock but can be destroyed by hot water, what am I?

35. The more you take away, the bigger I get. What am I?

36. I have the ability to run, but I do not have legs. What am I?

37. What has the ability to go around the world without leaving its corner?

38. What has plenty of keys but is not able to open any locks?

39. What tastes better than it smells?

40. I am an odd number. If you take away one letter, I will become even. What number am I?

41. What goes through cities and towns but never moves?

42. I will survive if you drop me from the tallest building in the world. However, I will die if you drop me into water. What am I?

43. What has a head and a tail but does not have a body?

44. What has an eye but cannot see?

45. Paul is six feet tall, works as an assistant at a butcher shop, and wears shoes that are 9 in size. What does Paul weigh?

46. What kind of tree can be carried in your hand?

47. What two things can never be eaten for breakfast?

48. What can get broken without ever being held?

49. What invention gives you the ability to look straight through a solid wall?

50. What can be caught but not thrown?

51. What is right at the end of a rainbow?

52. What is as light as a feather but can't be held by the strongest man for more than a few minutes?

53. You are given a pound of bricks and a pound of feathers. Which weighs more?

54. I belong to you, but your friends and family use me more than you do. What am I?

55. What has a neck but does not have a head?

56. If you look at my face, you will not find the number 13. What am I?

57. What question can you never say yes to?

58. What is the Capital in France?

59. What is right in front of you all the time but cannot be seen?

60. What animal is striped, black, white, and blue?

61. Where will you be able to find cities, towns, roads, and buildings, but no people?

62. What must be broken before it can be used?

63. What begins with the t, ends with t, and contains t?

64. If you do not keep me to yourself, I will break. What am I?

65. What can you always count on when things go wrong?

66. When Sally was 6, her sister was half of her age. Sally is currently 60 years old. How old would that make her sister?

67. You draw one line on a page. How do you make it longer without touching it?

68. What is difficult to get out of but easy to get into?

69. Mary has five daughters, and each daughter has a brother. How many children does Mary have?

70. David's parents have three children. Snap and Crackle are two of their names, but what is the third child's name?

71. You buy me for dinner, but you do not actually eat me. What am I?

72. How many months have 28 days in them?

73. What has four legs but can't walk?

74. How can 6 be made into an odd number?

75. I can be both a liquid and a solid. I bubble and can be found in most homes. What am I?

76. I have various emotions and expressions. What am I?

77. What type of bee can be passed around without causing any pain?

78. I can go up or down. I can be both curvy or straight. What am I?

79. I can be both major or minor. What am I?

80. Why don't celebrities sweat?

81. I shave every day, but my beard stays the exact same length. What am I?

82. You notice a boat filled with plenty of people. However, there isn't one single person. How can this be possible?

83. A man passed away from old age on his 26th birthday. How could this be possible?

84. I have branches, but no leaves or fruit. What am I?

85. What can reply but can't talk?

86. I follow you everywhere and copy every single move that you make. However, you cannot hold or touch me. What am I?

87. What can I hold in my right hand but not in my left?

88. What can never be put in a pot?

89. If you are running a race and you pass the person in third place, what place will you be in?

90. What has plenty of eyes but cannot see anything?

91. Which band never plays any music?

92. What has words but does not say anything?

93. What has plenty of teeth but cannot eat?

94. What has four fingers and a thumb but does not have a hand?

95. Where does one wall meet another?

96. Which type of building has many stories?

97. What has 13 hearts but does not have any other organs?

98. What has flies and 4 wheels?

99. Two is company and three is a crowd. What are four and five?

100. Three doctors claim that Steven is their brother. However, when asked about it, Steven claims to have no brothers. How is this possible?

101. Two fathers and two sons are driving in a car. However, there are only three people in the vehicle. How is this possible?

102. What can be found in the middle of Toronto?

103. I am the start of everything and the end of everywhere. I am the start of eternity and the end of time and space. What am I?

104. When you read me forwards, I am not heavy. However, when you read me backward, I am. What word am I?

105. What word is 3/7 chicken, ⅔ cat, and 2/4 goat?

106. What is the end of everything?

107. Which one word is pronounced exactly the same with five letters as it is with one?

108. What can fill an entire room but take up no space?

109. The more of me that you take, the more of me that you leave behind. What am I?

110. If I turn once, you will not get in. If I turn twice, you will not get out. What am I?

111. I can be made, saved, and spent. What am I?

112. What breaks and never falls?

113. What falls and never breaks?

114. If I am not fed, I will die. However, everything I touch turns red. What am I?

115. The person who makes me has no use for me. The person who buys me will never use me. The person who uses me will never feel me. What am I?

116. What type of cheese is made backward?

117. Why did the girl bury her torch?

118. Which letter contains the most water?

119. What starts with 'p', ends with 'e' and contains thousands of letters?

120. Why would a woman living in England not be buried in Ireland?

121. Four men are in a canoe. However, when it capsizes, only three men get their hair wet. How is this possible?

122. What type of ship has two mates but no captain?

123. John throws a ball. The ball returns, even though it doesn't hit anybody or anyone. How is this possible?

124. An electric train is moving South. Which way is the smoke moving?

125. I come out at night without being called. However, I am lost during the day without having been stolen. What am I?

126. Why do lions only eat raw meat?

127. What can go up but can never come back down?

128. Why did Mickey Mouse decide to go to space?

129. If you throw a grey stone in the Red Sea, what would it become?

130. What letter can make 'one' disappear?

131. What does an island have in common with the letter 't'?

132. Which three consecutive days are not names of days of the week?

133. Why are teddy bears never hungry?

134. What is the best way to cure dandruff?

135. A man does not have all of his fingers on one hand. What is he called?

136. Which drink does an invisible man enjoy the most?

137. I do not have eyes, ears, or a tongue. However, I can see, hear, and taste everything. What am I?

138. I can fly, even though I do not have wings. I can cry, even though I do not have eyes. What am I?

139. I am not alive, yet I can die. What am I?

140. I was created big. However, I slowly become shorter and shorter as time passes. What am I?

141. I do not have legs, but if you keep me warm, I will eventually walk away. What am I?

142. A bird and a squirrel are racing to the top of a coconut tree. Who will get to the orange first?

143. You throw away the outside and cook the inside. Afterward, you eat the outside and throw away the inside. What is it?

144. Even though I have been around for millions of years, I am no more than a month old. What am I?

145. Poor people have this. Rich people need this. If you eat it, you will soon pass away. What is it?

146. I am a location that is round on both sides and 'hi' in the middle. Where am I?

147. I have four eyes, but I cannot see. What am I?

148. I come down, but I never go back up. What am I?

149. Even though you can serve me, you can never eat me. What am I?

150. I can clap, even though I do not have any hands. What am I?

151. What always sleeps with shoes on?

152. What animal has the ability to honk without having a horn?

153. You are in a dark cabin with a match, a candle, a fireplace, and a lantern. Which do you light first?

154. How far can a dog run into the forest?

155. What was the highest mountain in the world before Mt. Everest was discovered by people?

156. A plane crash lands on the border of Spain and France. Where would the survivors be buried?

157. Even though I cannot tell the future, I am always able to predict the score of a football match before it starts. How is this possible?

158. A man walks into a bar, and the waitress greets him, "Good morning, Admiral." How could she possibly know that he was an Admiral?

159. A man arrives at a hotel, having pushed his car a few blocks, and tells the owner that he is bankrupt. Why does he do this?

160. Why are ghosts bad liars?

161. Imagine that you are in a room that is rapidly filling with water. More so, there are no windows or doors. How do you escape?

162. Why do bees hum?

163. What are you doing when your parachute won't open?

164. What can go up and down but can't move?

165. A young girl is sitting in a house alone at night. There are no lights or candles, meaning that the room is completely dark. However, she is reading. How is this possible?

166. In what way is Europe similar to a frying pan?

167. A car is traveling at 40 kilometers per hour into a very strong headwind. The surface of the road is also very rough and bumpy, heavily affecting the speed of the vehicle. With all of this in mind, how long will it take the car to travel 40 kilometers?

168. A bus driver is moving in the opposite direction to all of the cars passing by. A police officer drives past the driver but does not stop or try to arrest him. Why is this?

169. What sort of money is used by vampires?

170. What do you get when you cross an elephant with a fish?

171. I can come in multiple colors. When I get too full, I will burst. What am I?

172. I can be big, white, dirty or wicked. What am I?

173. I can be round or oval in shape. I can be either light or dark. What am I?

174. What do you get when you cross a vampire and a snowman?

175. How can eight 8's be added to get 1000?

176. There are 5 apples on a table, and you take away three. How many do you have left?

177. What do the numbers 11, 69, and 88 have in common?

178. You have a very large money box that is roughly 15 inches wide and 5 inches tall. How many coins can you put in the empty box?

179. Mr. Smith has two children. If the one child is a boy, what are the odds of the second child also being a boy?

180. I can be multiplied by any other number, but the answer will always be the same. What number am I?

181. If four people can fix four cars in four hours, how many cars can be fixed by eight people in eight hours?

182. A little boy was rushed to the hospital after falling off his bike. However, the doctor said, "I cannot treat this boy as he is my son." However, the doctor was not the boy's father. How was this possible?

183. A girl fell off a 30-foot ladder. However, she did not get hurt. How is this possible?

184. What is always late and never present right now?

185. Why do birds fly south during the winter?

186. How do dog catchers earn money?

187. A man rides into a small village on Monday, stays for two days, and leaves on Monday. How is this possible?

188. How many animals were taken on the ark by Moses?

189. I move very slowly around your garden. Perhaps it is my shell that weighs me down. What am I?

190. I can jump and climb very well. You are most likely scared of me, and I can be found in most homes. I have the ability to build my own house, and I make it much larger than necessary. What am I?

191. I can be heard better at night. I have four legs, but I do not have a tail. What am I?

192. I am known as a King. It's hard to tame me, and I am often seen as the fiercest of them all. What am I?

193. How do you get to Carnegie Hall?

194. What year is a frog's favorite?

195. What can you find at the end of a line?

196. How is it possible for a man to go 10 days with no sleep?

197. What type of fruit is always unhappy?

198. What gets sharper when used a lot?

199. What is a mummy's favorite food?

200. What can be heard but not seen or touched?

201. What number has all of its letters in alphabetical order when spelled?

202. What do teenagers say when they struggle with even numbers?

203. I have plenty of wheels, but I do not move. What am I?

204. I am an article of clothing that sounds like the upper part of a war machine. What am I?

205. What book do teachers not recommend?

206. If there is a rooster sitting on a roof and it lays an egg, which way would the egg roll?

207. A single-story house has a red bookcase, a red painting, a red carpet, a red sofa, and a red table. What color is the staircase?

208. What do the Atlantic and Indian ocean say to each other?

209. What is the easiest way to double your money?

210. What can shatter if dropped, but will smile back at you if you do to it?

211. Which word is always spelled incorrectly?

212. Which animal has a horn but does not make any noise?

213. What is as big as an elephant but weighs nothing?

214. Even though my pockets are empty, they have something in them. What is it?

215. I fly all day. However, I go nowhere. What am I?

216. I get whipped and beaten. However, I do not cry. What am I?

217. I do not have legs, but I can move very fast. I cannot see very well, but I can sense you. What am I?

218. I am known as the wisest animal around. What am I?

219. I am the most dangerous and destructive creature in the world. What am I?

220. What is a rabbits' favorite music?

221. What makes a cat the perfect soldier?

222. Why do turkeys get very full on thanksgiving?

223. Dogs have fleas. What do sheep have?

224. What color socks are worn by bears?

225. What is the worst animal to play poker with?

226. What type of egg is laid by an evil chicken?

227. I have big ears, big feet, and soft fur. What am I?

228. I have scales all over and can change color depending on my surroundings. What am I?

229. I am a land animal who lives in trees. I am part of the cat family, but you cannot keep me as a pet. What am I?

230. I am a bird, but I love the ocean. What am I?

231. Sally has three brothers: Matthew, Scott, and Finn. What is the fourth sibling's name?

232. How does a man cross a river without getting wet?

233. I have four legs and am soft in the middle. What am I?

234. I have hundreds of legs but cannot stand on my own. Although my neck is so long, I do not have a head. What am I?

235. All I can do is point, yet I guide men all over the world. What am I?

236. I am lovely and round and can be discovered in the ocean. What am I?

237. I am circular in shape, yet I have no center. What am I?

238. I am the tallest of all animals. What am I?

239. I live in darkness and cannot see. However, I can sense movement from miles away. What am I?

240. What do you call bears with no ears?

241. Which bird species can carry the most weight?

242. What is an insect's favorite sport?

243. Why are frogs always happy?

244. Why did the picture go to jail?

245. What kind of hair do oceans have?

246. What is brown and sticky?

247. What do prisoners use to call each other?

248. What object only starts working once it is fired?

249. Which type of nails do carpenters hate to hit?

250. What do lawyers wear to court?

251. Why did the scarecrow win the Nobel prize?

252. What is the coldest country in the world?

253. What is the longest word?

254. What is a man at the top of a hill called?

255. What invention gives you the power to walk through walls?

256. Two waves had a race. Who won?

257. Why did the house go to the doctor?

258. What did the blanket say to the bed?

259. What has two hands and a face, but no fingers or eyes?

Answers

Long Riddles

1. The Sri Lankan housekeeper was lying and stole the captain's valuables. He claimed that the Japanese flag was upside down, but because the flag is just a circle, there is no right-way up.

2. The third man would know the color of his hat. The third man knows that there are just two caps of each color. If the fourth man sees two caps of the same color ahead of him, he would understand that his hat is the opposite. Since the caps alternate in color, this man would only have a 50% chance of getting his hat color right, meaning that he would not say anything. The third man understands why the fourth man remains silent, guessing that it must mean that the two hats in front of him are opposite colors. With this in mind, the third man knows that his hat color is the opposite of the hat color in front of him.

3. Sarah did not hang up the phone after her friend had called. Therefore, the friend was able to hear the entire conversation between Sarah and the thief, alerting the authorities.

4. The third son purchased a match.

5. Simon died from carbon dioxide poisoning. Since the pole was 6' long and as wide as a quarter, the air exhaled by Simon would not make it out of the pole before Simon breathed in again. In other words, Simon would eventually just be breathing in Carbon Dioxide. Since Paul was a Doctor, he would have known about the risk of poisoning, meaning that he told Simon to use the pole for breathing to kill him on purpose.

6. John put 2 pounds in the one bag, 3 pounds in the second, and 11 pounds in the third. Afterward, he placed the second bag in the third bag and the first bag in the second bag. Since the bags felt the weight that they each carried, they inaccurately gave the message 23 pounds were taken.

7. Brav, The Bold, won the contest. Gringo The Gorgeous could not have won because the champion was not a child of the King (both of the winner's parents were celebrated at the ceremony). Abner's only weapon was a spatha (or sword), meaning that he could also not be the champion. Igor, The Terrible, killed 4 with his ax and 5 with his spear - he could not have been the champion, as the winner killed half a dozen dragons with his ax alone. Victor could not have been the champion as he did not have a horse - the winner's horse was celebrated at the party. This means that Brav is the only option.

8. The full moon diminishes with time, while the quarter moon grows and becomes brighter over time.

9. Matthew told Mike to get in his wheelbarrow, meaning that Mike would not be able to start at the same time as Matthew. By this logic, Matthew would automatically win.

10. The German man owns the fish.

11. He can suggest that he takes 98 pieces of treasure for himself and that the third and fifth pirates take one piece each. If there were only two men, the younger of the two would deny the suggestion in order to take all of the gold for himself. If there were three men, the first man to suggest a plan could offer the other two one piece of treasure each and keep the rest for himself as the second man would not get anything if he were to propose an idea. If there were 4 men, the first man to go could offer the youngest pirate one piece of treasure and keep the rest for himself - the youngest pirate would agree to this plan as he would not receive any gold in the next plan. With this being said, the third and fifth pirate would agree to receive one piece of gold as they would not receive anything in the next plan.

12. The King gave all of the children fake seeds, meaning that the little girl who showed up with an empty pot was the only child who did not lie.

13. The mailman stole the one hundred thousand dollars because he could not have hidden the envelope in-between the second and third pages. (The first and second pages are on opposite sides to the third page)

14. The wife said, "What is this?"

15. The twenty-seven dollars plus the three dollars kept by the guests add up to thirty dollars.

16. The man wearing the baseball cap made a bet for money with the man wearing a cowboy hat first, claiming that he would be able to make the bartender laugh after spraying the restaurant with water.

17. The swan must travel a quarter of the way to land and then swim in a circular path - since she has to travel a shorter distance to make a complete rotation, she will move faster than the dog and be able to put distance in between them. Once the swan is as far away from the dog as possible, she must swim to the land. She will then be able to fly away before the dog reaches her.

18. The real parents are the second couple.

19. The passage states that every 'single' person passed away in the plane crash. In other words, no couples were affected.

20. Johnny should not take any bet and return home with the three hundred dollars that he was sent to pick up.

21. The boy uses boiled eggs for the spinning competitions. If he used raw eggs, the maid would hand him a mop instead of a broom.

22. Tommy could ask both guards, "Would the other guard say that this tunnel leads to the land of punishment?"

23. The men could use the match to start their own fire near the cliff. They could then use the water to put it out, leaving them surrounded by burnt forest material. The fire would not be able to burn that area again, meaning that the men would be safe as long as they stayed in the previously burnt region while the fire passed through.

24. The travel company knew that Jack was guilty because he had only bought one return ticket from Croatia, meaning that he was not planning on returning with his wife.

25. As soon as the Grim Reaper left, the youngest son went to the candle and blew it out. This way, the wick of the candle never burned out, meaning that the Reaper would break his promise if he were to return.

Shorter Riddles

1. The electric chair because you know that the power is out

2. The spy gave the answer '5'. The answer is based on how many letters are in the number called out by the guard.

3. The messy barber would have to get his hair done by the clean barber and vice versa. This would mean that the messy barber does a better job.

4. The mule because the gold would've been way too heavy for the men to carry.

5. Taking out the small loan and storing her car at the bank was cheaper than paying for long-term parking at the airport.

6. Steven 'was' the strongest man in the world - in other words, he is no longer the strongest man.

7. Michael already has one cat, meaning that he would have one more than the teacher.

8. Make six people sit on one side of the see-saw, and six people sit on the other side. You must then take the six men who weighed more and divide

them randomly into groups of three. These two groups will have to sit on either side of the see-saw - one side, again, will be heavier. The heavier group must be divided into two groups of one, with each man sitting on either side of the see-saw.

There are three scenarios that could occur: one side could be heavier, the other side could be heavier, or they could both weigh the same. The man on the heavier side would be the man who has a different weight. If they both weighed the same, the third man from the group of three who did not sit on the see-saw is the man who weighs more.

9. The man knocked on her front door. If he really believed that it was his room, he would not have knocked.

10. The neighbor gave the boys an extra cow, making the total 18. This meant that the oldest brother would receive 9, the middle brother would receive 6, and the youngest brother would receive 2. However, since this total is only 17, the neighbor could take his cow back.

11. Surlamina was the kidnapper of the son. There is no Secretary of State in a monarchy, meaning that there are no 'Secretary of State duties' for her to complete. In other words, she lied about her whereabouts when interrogated by the Queen.

12. The philosopher wound his clock to a random time before leaving for his friend's house. Even though it was not the correct time, he could use the clock to measure the elapsed time. He then checked his friend's clock when he arrived and before he left to walk home. Once he gets home, he could check to see how long he had been gone for. For example, if he set

the clock to 9 before he left and it now read 10, it would mean that he had been gone for 13 hours. If his friend's clock read 10 when he arrived and 9 20 when he left, it would mean that he had been gone for 11 hours and 20 minutes. If the time elapsed on his clock was 12 hours, it would mean that he has been walking for 40 minutes. However, since he walked to his friend's house and from it, he would actually have been walking for 20 minutes each way. Therefore, the actual time would be 9:20 + 20 minutes or 9:40.

13. A tombstone

14. The maid was guilty. She had told the parents that she was busy cleaning the corners of the house while they were out, but, since the hose was round, it did not have any corners.

15. The man would have to take the rabbit across to the other side of the river first. He would then return to collect the lettuce. However, instead of simply leaving the lettuce on the side with the rabbit, he leaves the lettuce and collects the rabbit again. When he returns to the side with the fox, he would drop the rabbit off and collect the fox. Lastly, after dropping the fox off on the side with the lettuce, he would have to go back and collect the rabbit once more.

16. Adam could freeze some ice in an ice tray. If the ice is still in the tray when he returns, his meat will be safe to eat. However, if he returns and the ice has melted (in other words, the ice tray is empty), his freezer will need to be cleaned out.

17. In the dark, the girl unknowingly placed the large rock on her long dress, preventing her from running away. She then literally died of fear.

Quick Riddles

1.   Noon

2.   A mongoose

3.   A towel

4.   Two. A sheep has hooves, and a dog has paws.

5.   A telephone

6.   Wrong

7.   I C U

8.   In Finland

9.   An umbrella

10.   In the dictionary

11.   A sponge

12.   A plant

13.   The letter 'r'

14.   Less

15.   Your word

16.   Earth

17.   A railing

18.   A bed

19.   A goose

20.   A pair of gloves

21.   Light

22.   A pillow

23.   A dress

24.   February - it is the shortest month.

25.   A fence

26.   A matchstick

27.   An ice cube

28.   A priest

29.   A chalkboard

30.   An anchor

31.   A clock

32. Darkness

33. An echo

34. An ice cube

35. A hole

36. A nose

37. A stamp

38. A piano

39. A tongue

40. Seven

41. Roads

42. A piece of paper

43. A coin

44. A needle

45. Meat

46. A palm

47. Lunch and dinner

48. A promise

49. A window

50. A cold

51. The letter 'w'

52. His breath

53. They both weigh a pound

54. Your name

55. A bottle

56. A clock

57. Are you asleep?

58. The letter 'F'

59. The future

60. A sad zebra

61. A map

62. An egg

63. A teapot

64. A promise

65. Your hands

66. 57 years old

67. You draw a shorter line next to it

68. Trouble

69. 6 - each sister has the same brother

70. David

71. Utensils

72. All of them

73. A table

74. If you remove the letter 's', you will be left with 'ix'. IX is the number 9 in Roman numerals.

75. Soap

76. Emojis

77. A frisbee

78. A staircase

79. Piano keys

80. They have plenty of fans

81. A barber

82. All the people are couples (in other words, they all have a significant other)

83. He was born on the 29th of February

84. A bank

85. An echo

86. A shadow

87. My left hand

88. It's lid

89. Third place

90. A potato

91. A rubber band

92. A book

93. A comb

94. An empty glove

95. In the corner

96. A library

97. A deck of cards

98. A garbage truck

99. Nine

100. Steven has three sisters

101. There is a grandfather, father, and son in the car

102. The letter 'o'

103. The letter 'e'

104. Not

105. The word 'Chicago'

106. The letter 'g'

107. Queue

108. Light

109. Footsteps

110. A key

111. Money

112. Day

113. Night

114. Fire

115. A coffin

116. Edam

117. The battery dies

118. The letter 'c'

119. The post office

120. Because she is still living

121. The one man is bald

122. A relationship

123. He throws the ball up into the air

124. There is no smoke because the train is electric

125. Stars

126. Because they never learned how to cook

127. Your age

128. He wanted to visit Pluto

129. It would become wet

130. The letter 'g'

131. It is surrounded by water

132. Yesterday, today, and tomorrow

133. They are always stuffed

134. To shave your hair

135. Normal - all of your fingers should be spread on both of your hands

136. Evaporated milk

137. A brain

138. A cloud

139. A battery

140. A candle

141. A chicken

142. Neither the bird nor the squirrel - it is a coconut tree, not an orange tree.

143. Corn on the cob

144. The moon

145. Nothing

146. Ohio

147. Mississippi

148. Rain

149. A tennis ball

150. Thunder

151. A horse

152. A goose

153. The match

154. Halfway. Once he gets further than halfway, he will be running out of the forest

155. Mt.Everest - the mountain has always been the highest in the world, even before it was discovered.

156. They would not be buried as they were still alive

157. The score of a football match is always the same at the start (0 - 0)

158. He was wearing his uniform

159. He is playing Monopoly

160. You can see straight through them

161. Stop imagining

162. They do not know the words

163. Jumping to conclusions

164. The temperature

165. She is blind and is able to read braille

166. Greece is at the bottom

167. An hour

168. The bus driver is walking instead of driving

169. Blood Money

170. Swimming trunks

171. A balloon

172. A lie

173. A potato

174. Frostbite

175. $888 + 88 + 8 + 8 + 8 = 1000$

176. You take away 3, so you will have 3

177. They can be read the same when written upside down

178. You can only put in one before the money box is no longer empty

179. 50%

180. Zero

181. 16 cars

182. The doctor was the boy's mother

183. She was standing on the bottom step of the ladder when she fell

184. Later

185. It's too far for them to walk

186. By the pound

187. His horse's name is Friday

188. None. They were taken on the ark by Noah

189. A snail

190. A spider

191. A frog

192. A lion

193. Practice, practice, practice

194. A leap year

195. The letter 'e'

196. He sleeps at night

197. A blueberry

198. Your brain

199. A wrap

200. Your voice

201. Forty

202. 'I can't even'

203. A parking lot

204. A tank top

205. Facebook

206. Roosters can't lay eggs

207. It is a single-story house - there is no staircase

208. They don't say anything - they just wave

209. With a mirror

210. A mirror

211. The word incorrectly

212. A rhino

213. An elephant's shadow

214. Holes

215. A flag

216. An egg

217. A snake

218. An elephant

219. A human

220. Hip hop

221. It has 9 lives

222. They get stuffed

223. Fleece

224. None - they have bear feet

225. A cheetah

226. A deviled egg

227. A rabbit

228. A chameleon

229. A leopard

230. A seagull

231. Sally

232. The lake is frozen

233. A bed

234. A broom

235. A compass

236. A pearl

237. A ring

238. A giraffe

239. A bat

240. 'Ears'

241. A crane

242. Cricket

243. They eat what bugs them

244. It was framed

245. Wavy

246. A stick

247. Cellphones

248. A rocket

249. Fingernails

250. Lawsuits

251. He was outstanding in his field

252. Chili

253. Smiles

254. Cliff

255. A door

256. The tied

257. It has a window pain

258. I got you covered

259. A clock

Printed in Great Britain
by Amazon

56159091R00050